God Speaks...
Diary of
Spirt-Led
Devotions

By

Gia Clunie

Holy Fire Publishing
Oak Ridge, TN

The Books of Matthew and Luke, New King James Version, Copyright 1982, Thomas Nelson, Inc./NELSON

The Books of Jeremiah and Psalms, Holy Bible. New Living Translation, Copyright 1996, Tyndale House Publishing

The Books of Psalms, Proverbs and Jeremiah, The Message, Copyright 2001, Eugene H. Peterson /NavPress

The Books of Matthew, Job, Acts, Ephesians and Genesis, New American Standard, Copyright 1995, The Lockman Foundation

The Books of Mark, 1 and 2 Corinthians, Ecclesiastes, Ephesians, James, Psalms, Matthew, John, Exodus, Ruth, Amos, Isaiah, Nehemiah and Romans, New International Version, Copyright 1984, International Bible Society/Zondervan

The Books of John, Psalms, Revelations and Leviticus, Amplified Bible, Copyright 1987, The Lockman Foundation/Zondervan

Copyright © 2004 Gia Clunie

All rights reserved. No part of this publication may be reproduced, stored in a retrieval system, or transmitted in any form or by any means, electronic, mechanical, photocopying, recording, or otherwise, without the prior written permission of the publisher.

Published by:
Holy Fire Publishing
P.O. Box 5192, Oak Ridge, TN 37831-5192
www.christianpublish.com

ISBN: 0-9761112-2-5

Printed in the United States of America and the United Kingdom

Dedication Page

I would like to dedicate this book to my son, Bryant Richard McClary; whose life inspired me to have a relationship with my Holy Father.

Love,
Mommy

Table of Contents

Is it good to ya?	7
City on a Hill	9
Wake Up	11
Shatter the Devil	12
R.A.I.N	14
3 P's	16
3 = 1	18
Do Over	22
Trees	25
An Introduction into Humility	27
It's a Different World	29
Part Time Christian	32
Karate Kid	34
Tick…Tock	36
Seasons	38
Comfort	40
Amen!	42
Home Sweet Temple	44
Un-Veil-ed	46
The Glory of the New Covenant	48
Spring Cleaning	50
All Worship…No Worry	52
Fireplace	54
Back Seat Driver	56
HOPE	58
King's Kid	60
Go Home!	62
Show and Tell	64
Recall	66
Desiring God's Desires	68
Characteristics	70
Love Thy Neighbor	73
Walking with Armour	75

Is it good to ya?

James 4:1 -3 What causes fights and quarrels among you? Don't they come from your desires that battle within you? You want something but don't get it. You kill and covet, but you cannot have what you want. You quarrel and fight. You do not have, because you do not ask God. When you ask, you do not receive, because you ask with wrong motives, that you may spend what you get on your pleasures.

I would say that I have been battling with why others have what I want. I couldn't understand why I was still without certain things and it seemed like those around me, saved or not, were just sitting in the pot of gold.

To say the least God convicted me for having those thoughts.

When I read the above verse, God pointed out to me that I don't have because I don't ask Him and I don't receive because I ask with the wrong motives – that I may spend what I get on my pleasures…

I know that there have been times that I've prayed for my finances and when I get a little bit of change in my pocket, I immediately spend it on frivolous things; never once did I think to tithe it. HE convicted me on my heart when I ask for things, is it because somebody else has it or is it something that I truly need/want? HE told me to stop looking at what others have, because HE has my blessings in store for me. And it's only when HE sees fit to give it, that I will receive it.

HE also told me that there are things that HE wants to bless me with but I am not asking HIM for it. I said to HIM…I don't want to treat you like Santa Claus. HE said: Trust ME, I am not going to give anything to you that you don't need to have in your life, *just* because you asked for it.

I heard Heavy D's song "Is it good to ya" on the radio and although it is a secular song with a different meaning, HE said "Am I not good to ya, do I not supply your every need, Am I not there when you need someone to cry to? **AM I NOT GOOD TO YA?!**" I was driving and crying! Then a song by Aretha Franklin came on and all I really heard was a part that she says "count your blessings"! HE said if you sat down to count your blessings, you would never get back up! HE said the mere fact that you *can count your blessings* is a blessing! Praise God!

Psalms 37:11 But the meek shall inherit the land and enjoy great peace.

Be Blessed,
Gia

City on a Hill

Matthew 5:14 -16
"You are the light of the world. A city on a hill cannot be hidden. Neither do people light a lamp and put it under a bowl. Instead they put it on its stand, and it gives light to everyone in the house. In the same way, let your light shine before men, that they may see your good deeds and praise your Father in heaven.

How many of you have seen yourselves as the 'city on the hill?' You are noticed from afar!

How many times have you taken a trip somewhere and you look out into the city and you immediately admire what is **SITTING HIGH** and you say to yourself 'now that's a nice house'. Although it's in the midst of so much, it appears to stand out from it surroundings/ the world.

Where God has you, the enemy cannot touch you. All you have to do is *turn on your light* and call on your Father. All He has to do is reach His hand down and cover you with His unconditional love. Have you noticed that He has you up on a hill close to His bosom…close to His heart?

The enemy can see you from a distance. He sees that you exist, but he can't get to you.

Everywhere you go, the light of God is shining in you. No matter how the enemy may try to attack…whether it's in your marriage, health, finances, job, family or even driving in traffic…*anything* the enemy tries to do to dim that light, he will soon find out it is **impossible.** The **light** is everlasting! It represents the Holy Spirit, His son Jesus Christ and God himself!

The next time you wonder why that person is staring at you…know that they are admiring the 'city on the hill'….

Be Blessed,
Gia

Wake Up!

John 11:43 – 44 When he had said this, Jesus called in a loud voice, "Lazarus, come out!" The dead man came out, his hands and feet wrapped with strips of linen, and a cloth around his face. Jesus said to them, "Take off the grave clothes and let him go."

Dead issues = issues that are not representing the Holy Spirit.

HE said it's time to wake them up, bring them from the dead. As long as you go day to day holding onto 'death' you can not prosper. You have to speak life to that dead situation, raise it from the dead and operate in the Spirit.

Take off the grave clothes…All of the burdens, all of the negativity, all of the sorrow, all of the stress, all of the gossip, all of the hatred, all of the pride…**take it off!**
Don't let your spirit be clothed in all that represents the enemy!

If He can raise a man from the dead…there is nothing that He can't do! He went to a human being who was no longer breathing, had no visible sign of life and had been lying 'dead' for four days. The area was smelly to the point that Martha – Lazarus' sister – didn't even want to push the stone back…No matter what the situation was Jesus went to the grave sight and said 'Come out' and 'Take off your grave clothes.' Praise God!

Be Blessed,
Gia

Shatter the Devil

Exodus 15:6
"Your right hand, O LORD ,
was majestic in power.
Your right hand, O LORD ,
shattered the enemy.

When the enemy starts to prowl around in your life, you have to be determined not to let him beat you down.

The enemy will try to block out blessings that God has for you. He will try to convince you that God will not provide as He said He would. But as Christians, we have to turn a deaf ear to the LIAR!

God gave me the analogy of a car running over a bottle in the street and said crush him beneath your feet! Praise God!

God said don't give the enemy **ANYTHING** to thrive on, don't give him the opportunity to make a mountain out of a mole hill. We really have to be careful about what we let come out of our mouths into the spiritual real (Proverbs 13:3 He who guards his lips guards his life, but he who speaks rashly will come into ruin).

You have to keep your guard up at all time through prayer, fasting, studying and consecrating. The enemy will try to attack you through your friends, family, co-workers and people out in the streets. He'll place obstacles in your path that will look so huge that you begin to doubt what God can do.

Just think of the car and the bottle…a huge mass crushing something that is not significant at all!! The enemy doesn't stand a chance against God and His children! Hallelujah!

Be Blessed,
Gia

R.A.I.N

Ruth 3:18 Then Naomi said "Wait, my daughter, until you find out what happens. For the man will not rest until the matter is settled today."

Amos 3:7 Surely the Sovereign LORD does nothing without revealing his plan to his servants the prophets.

Isaiah 61:2 to proclaim the year of the LORD's favor and the day of vengeance of our God, to comfort all who mourn

Nehemiah 9:5 Stand up and praise the LORD your God, who is from everlasting to everlasting. Blessed be your glorious name, and may it be exalted above all blessing and praise.

I was trying to get the significance of the word 'rain'….because when it rains, I don't get upset about it. I can feel God covering us. HE hasn't left and wants us to know that even when it is cloudy and rainy, He is still blessing us.

Not to mention after the rain comes the rainbow (Gen. 9:13..sign of the covenant between God and people.)

Lev. 26:4-5 I will send you rain in its season, and the ground will yield its crops and the trees of the field their fruit. Your threshing will continue until grape harvest and the grape harvest will continue until planting, and you will eat all the food you want and live in the safety in your land.

Be Blessed,
Gia

3 P's

Matthew 11:28 Come to Me, all you who labor and are heavy laden, and I will give you rest.

The three P's that God has given me are **Peace, Patience and Persistence…**

Peace – serene; tranquility

Patience – good-natured tolerance of delay

Persistence – refusing to give up or let go

There have been times when I have gotten upset and shed a tear because of my life's circumstances. God will ask me why am I crying and I tell Him that I just don't understand why certain things have to take place and He said rest in My Name. At that moment, I dried the tears and said thank you Jesus.
He then gave me the 3 P's to live by….

Being a Christian, I have quickly learned that I cannot go through my daily walk without having these three words at the forefront of my mind (spiritual and carnal). I have also noticed the enemy doesn't want me to obtain any of these qualities, because that will mean that he doesn't stand a chance…He is not going to disturb my serene life. He is not going to make me anxious and he is not going to make me give up on God's spoken WORD.

I have discovered that the enemy attacks because he knows what God has for me and he wants me to get discouraged and distracted from His promise.

God wants you to put these words into your memory bank…DON'T GIVE UP is what He is saying.

I pray that we all endure the storm. I pray that we speak to the mountains in our lives and lift our hands to Jesus and say, "Thank you!" REJOICE now and find rest in His Name.

Psalm 57:1 In the shadow of Your wings I will make my refuge, until these calamities have passed by…

Keep your eyes on Him and do it with a smile because the storm will not last always.

Be Blessed,
Gia

3 = 1
Try, Trials and Test = Triumphs…..

Try – Subject to trial or test, as to determine strength or effect

Trial – A source of distress that tests patience and endurance

Test – Procedure for critical evaluation

EQUALS

Triumph – rejoice over a victory

James 1:2 Consider it pure joy, my brothers, whenever you face **trials** of many kinds, because you know that the **testing of your faith** develops perseverance.
James 1:12 Blessed is the man who **perseveres under trial**, because when he has stood the test, **he will receive the crown of life** that God has promised to those who love him.

The Lord gave me the title **3=1** as I was reading and meditating on the above verses.

On a scale from 1 -10 (1 being very weak and 10 being very strong), how do you think you rate when it comes to tests of faith?

On a scale from 1-10, how well do you think you make it through trials?

On a scale from 1-10, where does your strength rank when you are tried?

I can honestly say that my scores aren't all that superb, but my goal is to increase my ranking on each one with the Lord's help.

Being faced with those three harsh realities, the joy comes in knowing TRIUMPH is not far away. Knowing we will receive the crown of life that God has promised is more than enough incentive for us to increase our rankings.

I don't proclaim that the journey will be an easy one, but God is with us the whole time. **Genesis 24:40 says...**"He replied, 'The LORD , before whom I have walked, will send His angel with you and make your journey a success....

HE will do what???...."Make your journey a success"....TRIUMPH!
To put it simply, God is not going to leave us hanging. HE has a plan for each of us. Each of us has a purpose and HE will see that we fulfill our purpose here on earth, but the catch is we have to allow HIM to use us. That has been my problem. I have become complacent and easily pleased with where I am in my Christian walk. God is saying to me 'NOPE, I am not done' (HE nor me). HE has begun to remove all distractions so that I have no other choice but to focus on HIM.
The day that we professed the Lord as our Savior, we consequently relinquished the driver's seat to God. We yielded our lives, our thoughts and our ways of

being to God. We can not try to go back and say 'God I got this' because we know better and we DON'T! So if we can trust and have faith in HIM with some things, we can trust and have faith in HIM with **ALL** things…don't forget now that HE is God all by himself; HE got this!!

The thing is, it pleases HIM when we succeed, when we are victorious, when we come off the battlefield **<u>WALKING</u>** and not crawling, when we have defeated the devil!

 I am going off the subject, but God is leading me in another direction right now…
 I know each of you remember sitting in your 1st period class in high school on a Monday morning with a pop quiz in your face and you have absolutely no clue as to what the answers are. You immediately look up into the sky praying that the answers will fall onto your paper. But once you realize that that is not going to occur, you regretfully turn in your quiz with just your name and date on it. You leave out of the class feeling empty because you know the teacher is going to review what you have done, and your fear is what will the teacher think of me???
You knew that you should have been prepared for the quiz and the only way you could have been prepared is by studying…reading and meditating on the information the teacher is trying to equip you with for the future.
(the above story may just have been my own personal experience☺)

The Lord is trying to equip us with information that we will need in the future. We have to be more diligent in our reading, meditating and seeking.

While I was meditating on the Word, HE had me to look up the word 'mature'….
James 1:4 Perseverance must finish its work so that you may be **mature** and complete, not lacking anything…

MATURITY – reaching a desired or final condition; ripe…when I read the word ripe, The Lord said 'fruit'…fruit can be consumed in its mature stage…The Lord can consume us in our mature stage…so read the WORD!

Be Blessed,
Gia

Do Over!

Psalm 23
³ he **restores** my soul.
He guides me in paths of righteousness
for his name's sake.

Psalm 102
¹⁶ For the LORD will **rebuild** Zion
and appear in his glory.

Psalm 51
¹⁰ Create in me a pure heart, O God,
and **renew** a steadfast spirit within me.

Psalm 30
¹¹ You turned my wailing into dancing;
you **removed** my sackcloth and clothed me with joy.

Psalm 25
¹⁵ My eyes are ever on the LORD ,
for only he will **release** my feet from the snare.

Psalm 71
²³ My lips will shout for joy
when I sing praise to you-
I, whom you have **redeemed**.

I am sure that as a child, when you were playing with your friends, something might have occurred you didn't necessarily agree with…like you didn't kick the ball far enough, or you swung the bat as hard as you could and still missed the ball…so the first thing you hollered was DO OVER! And depending on what kind of friends you had, they might have *allowed* you to try again.

This morning, while I was in HIS presence, HE just started to throw all of the words that began with 're'…and HE said HE is a 'do over' GOD. HE hears our cries when we foul out. HE knows that we make mistakes and HE is such a gracious God that HE will grant us favor again and again and again….do you know of *anybody* other than GOD that will do such things??

So anyway, I began my search so that I could write the devotional, and I battled with it all day long. I searched the words that HE gave me and couldn't get anything, so I did a little quick prayer and asked God 'What am I supposed to be writing about?' Finally there was a breakthrough. I noticed that I could find each word in a verse in Psalms, knowing that King David wrote the majority of the Book of Psalms. What came to mind was that Jesus said that David was a man after HIS own heart…ooh-wee ☺. David knew that he could call on his HOLY FATHER when he did wrong and GOD would give him the revelation that HE would show favor in his life. HE is so wonderful!!!

HE loves us that much that HE will **REstore… REbuild… REnew… REdeem… REmove and RElease**…do you know *anybody* other than **GOD** that will do such things??

Now the last word that GOD gave me was
Rejoice….

Psalm 97
[12] **Rejoice** in the LORD , you who are righteous, and praise His holy name.

And HE even broke it down to me!   **Re-** do over; **joy** – exultant happiness….

REJOICE in **HIS** name over and over and over again…as **HE** shows us favor *over and over and over again!*

Be Blessed,
Gia

Trees

Proverbs 11:28 "A life devoted to things is a dead life, a stump; A **God-shaped life is a flourishing tree**."

Jeremiah 17:7-8 "Blessed are those who trust in the Lord…They are like trees planted along a riverbank, with roots that reach deep into the water. **Such trees are not bothered by the heat or worried by long months of drought**. Their leaves stay green, and they go right on producing delicious fruit."

Trees, trees, trees….Christians, Christians, Christians….do you see the correlation between TREES and CHRISTIANS?

A tree is to be planted.
HE first conceives the idea and chooses where HE will plant the tree.
HE gets a seed.
HE chooses a place that will be a place of nourishment for the tree.
HE chooses a place where the tree will provide a place of comfort for those who come around it.
HE waters the tree as it begins to grow up out of the ground.
HE prunes the branches and leaves.
HE watches the trees as it grows and produces fruit for others.
HE knows as the tree is flourishing above ground, it is also sprouting its roots beneath the surface.
HE knows as storms 'pass', the tree will **survive.**
HE knows every season that comes, the tree will **survive.**

A Christian is to be born.
God conceived our birth and chose where we would grow up.
HE gets a seed.
HE places us amongst friends and family who will assist in our growth in HIS word.
HE aligns our path, so that we can console other brothers and sisters with HIS word.
HE provides us with HIS word, so that we can learn and grow into a Christian.
HE molds our spirits to be 'like' HIS.
HE smiles upon HIS children as HE watches us become mature.
HE knows when rough times, bad times, crazy times and even un-explainable times occur, **we will remain standing**.
HE knows that we can withstand each and every change in our lives.

Roots = Grounded
Trunk= Growth
Branches= Stretching out in HIS WORD
Leaves = HIS WORD
Fruit = HIS final product=Us=Christians

Tree, tree, tree…..Christian, Christian, Christian…

Do you see the correlation between the two?! Amen.

Be Blessed,
Gia

An Introduction into Humility

Hello, my name is Gia and I am not perfect....

If more people introduced themselves in that manner, a lot of prideful spirits would be humbled.

Psalm 138:6 Though the Lord is great, He cares for the humble, but he keeps his distance from the proud.

Proverbs 16:18 Pride goes before destruction, and a haughty spirit before a fall.

Luke 14:11 For whoever exalts himself will be humbled, and he who humbles himself will be exalted.

The fact that my name is Gia and not Jesus should let you know right-away that I am not perfect and never should I carry myself as such. There are people (and some even being Christians) who tend to believe they are perfect, and carry themselves in that way.

There are some who believe because they have $.05 in their pocket while the person standing next to them only has $.03 in their pocket makes them a better person. Have they forgotten that true hospitality is giving to those who cannot repay (Luke 14:13-14)?

There are some that live in mansions while their brother has fallen on hard times and lives in a homeless shelter, and *they* believe they are better. Have they forgotten that he who has two coats should let his brother who has none, to have one (Luke 3:11)?

As I see it there is an answer to every question and every way of being in the Bible. As I see it ,Jesus, Son of God, is perfect. And even Jesus showed humility! Correct me if I am wrong but did Jesus go around 'popping his collar' when he performed a miracle??

How is it that we can get so beside ourselves that we can look down on our brothers and sisters? God loves us with all of our faults and shortcomings and He *still* chooses to show us favor!

Hello my name is_____ and I am not perfect!

In Psalms 138:6, it says that He keeps himself from those that are proud.
Can we truly take a chance on God stepping away from us?

In Proverbs 16:18, it says pride goes before destruction.
Do we really want to take a chance on bringing destruction into our lives?

And in Luke 14:11, it says that if we are humble, we are exalted.
Okay, I don't know about you, but I can stand to be exalted.

Hello, my name is_____, and I AM NOT PERFECT!

Yes, our blessings are plenty and it's not possible to list them all, but we can give back by showing kindness and generosity to those who cross our paths.

Are you getting it now?

Be Blessed,
Gia

It's a Different World

I can remember when I was graduating from high school and preparing myself to go to college. Many emotions were running through me at that time and it seemed as the day of leaving home drew near, I was really overwhelmed with anxiety. I had no idea what to expect and I knew that I wouldn't have my father there to correct me or pick me up when I fell. I was going to be on my own for the first time…well that's what I thought. Right before my departure, my father pulled me to the side to have the good ol' father-daughter speech, so I was gearing myself up for the 'study, study, study' speech. Well, he threw a curveball and said 'Don't get yourself into any compromising situations just to be somebody's friend'. And I am going to be honest; I didn't hear anything else that he said after that. But I can tell you that that one little phrase stuck in my head the **ENTIRE** time I was away at school.

My dad disliked very much for his children to disappoint him (the same as God). He would say that my behavior was a reflection of him (the same as God). Sometimes I used to think that it took a lot to carry the 'Clunie' name. And even during my moments of disobedience, I could always hear his voice in my head (the same as God).

As my natural father gave me that piece of advice; my Spiritual Father is saying the same thing to His people.

James 4:4….. Anyone who chooses to be a **friend** of the **world** becomes an enemy of God.

DON'T COMPROMISE WHO YOU ARE!

We are God's children; everything about us is a reflection of who He is. There is not a person out here who is 'that good' for us to disappoint our God and cause Him to consider us as an enemy. We can't afford that!

There was a time that a couple members of my family got into a 'discussion' about the James 4:4 verse. The reason why it came about is because we were flipping through the tv channels and there was an award show on. There were both gospel performers and secular performers. The first point that was made was that the gospel performers were being 'friends of the world' because they were performing at the show and the opposing point was the gospel performers could have been led to perform there because you never know who they may end up ministering to. As the 'discussion' was going on, my opinion was requested, and I didn't really know how to respond because I wasn't as familiar with the verse as they were.
But now that I am filled with Spirit, what I get from the verse is that God doesn't want us to choose to do anything that He hasn't requested us to do just to appease another, because our integrity or our God-like character will be under review. If at any time you are choosing to do something that is self-led and not God-led to satisfy another, you are compromising yourself – your Christianity.
The fact is - you will always find yourself ministering to someone somehow, but God won't have you to compromise who you are(who HE has you to be) in order to speak the WORD or to be the light in their lives.

God's World is a Different World from which we 'knew'.

Be Blessed,
Gia

Part Time Christian
Convenience or Consistent
1 Thessalonians 5:17
Pray without ceasing.

Ephesians 6:18
And pray in the Spirit on all occasions with all kinds of prayers and requests. With this in mind, be alert and always keep on praying for all the saints.

HOW DO YOU TREAT GOD?

Some of us are guilty of treating God like He is a 7-Eleven store around the corner.
We run to Him **ONLY** when we need something on-the-go.
God most definitely is not a convenience store and should not be treated like one.
If God decided to bless us in the same manner that we pray to Him…. where would we be?

Do we forget that HE is GOD…and if it wasn't for HIM *and* HIS gracious blessings, we would really be in a world of trouble???

The name of the game is **consistency**….praying in good and bad times, whether you are sitting on the mountain top or down in the valley**….pray on all occasions….**

Pray when you wake up in the morning with a roof over your head, with working limbs, a job to go to, clothes to put on your back, food to put in your stomach and even a bed to get out of.
Pray and say Thank you God, Thank you Jehovah-Jireh! YOU are the provider!

Pray for the deliverance that is needed in YOUR life.
Pray for wisdom, so that you can share the WORD with someone else.
Pray for obedience to His WORD.
Pray that He puts a hedge of protection around His children.
Pray for OTHERS!

God doesn't take ½ days off from fighting our battles....HE doesn't say 'ok its 5:00 now, I'm taking off'...He is not a Part Time God....**He is ALWAYS there!**

So why do we have banker's hours with Him???

Be Blessed,
Gia

Karate Kid

2 Timothy 2:15
Study to shew thyself approved unto God, a workman that needeth not to be ashamed, rightly dividing the word of truth.

One evening I was driving home and I was thinking about those I know who can quote scriptures verbatim and those that can give a background on a situation that occurred in the Bible, and said to God "I want to be like that; Why am I not like that now? I know I have to study the WORD, but I don't ever think that I can be at that point where scriptures just simply roll off my tongue.

At that moment HE gave me the movie Karate Kid (now I know it was HIM, b/c I hadn't thought about that movie in ages; almost forgot that it was ever made). HE gave me the scene where Daniel is cleaning Mr. Miyagi's car and painting the fence and said 'There's a process to everything'. Mr. Miyagi had Daniel doing little tedious projects to build Daniel up to be the best in martial arts. The whole time Daniel whined and griped because he thought he wasn't learning anything and couldn't benefit from what Mr. Miyagi had him doing….until that ONE DAY…Mr. Miyagi challenged Daniel to put all the work he had been doing into practice. Soon Daniel was able to see for himself that all along Mr. Miyagi was prepping him for competition…prepping him to be victorious!

Now, I can't even believe that I remember that movie and I am even more shocked that it has some relevance to those who are in the beginning of their Christian Walk (or even those that have been doing it for some time).

I understand now that God is prepping me for what's to come. I understand now that as long as I am diligent and pressing on, that I will be who God has called me to be.

Far as I know, God knew me before Larry and Narissa knew me. God paved the way for me before I even knew that I was going to yield my life to HIM….so why wouldn't I be the woman that HE has called for me to be? Why am I doubting my abilities…why am I putting limits on what I can do…LORD JESUS, HE has brought me to a place *already* that I never thought I would be….HIS word says that He is able to do exceedingly and abundantly above all that we can ask or think…THANK YOU GOD! Within a year, He has already proven Himself to me…I would have never thought of myself as He thinks of me. He is saying to me 'Let me do this, let me run things because I am about to blow your mind', My God, My God….

All I have to say is Bless God for ordaining our paths and calling us to be great people, because I know for a fact that I wouldn't have ever considered *this* for myself.

Be Blessed,
Gia

Tick…Tock

Ecclesiastes
3:1 There is a time for everything,
and a season for every activity under heaven

3:3…a time to kill and a time to heal,
a time to tear down and a time to build,

God laid Ecc. 3:3 on my heart, and every time I read it, I knew God was speaking to me but I couldn't quite get what God was trying to share with me.

HE said Tick-Tock, the enemy's time is up! HE said all that the enemy has had his hands on is **now and forever** released.

We as Christians are coming upon our breakthrough. I am not speaking merely of materialistic things, but what I would call soul-blessings…the purposes that HE has for our lives.
We will begin to operate more in the Spirit and less in the flesh.
The enemy has had his crafty way of making us think that we can't do what God has spoken, that we aren't good enough, that we aren't intelligent enough to do God's work…TICK-TOCK DEVIL, your time is UP! Hallelujah!

The time is now to **kill** all that represents the enemy.
The time is now to **heal** our minds, bodies and souls.
The time is now to **tear** down the enemies plots.
The time is now to **build** up our ministries.
The time is now to **WALK** IN GOD'S GLORY!!!!!!

TICK – TOCK….

God brought back to my remembrance a conversation that some co-workers and I were having. We were talking about children and how they can become impatient and one of my co-workers said that her niece sat in front of the clock one day waiting on 7:00 to arrive. My co-worker told her niece that the longer you sit in front of the clock, the longer it will take for time to pass by.
God said we have been sitting in front of the clock long enough, we have been asking "Lord when?" long enough. HE said step away from the clock!!
HE said stop worrying, wondering and contemplating…..because **He** doesn't break promises….HE said it and its DONE!

I want everybody who reads this to stand up and tell the enemy that he is now beneath your feet where he belongs…. tell him to stay down there on his belly… You let him know that he is not **worthy** enough to walk up-right… ….HALLELUJAH!!

TICK – TOCK ENEMY, YOUR TIME IS UP!

Be Blessed,
Gia

Seasons

Psalm 1
[3] **He is like a tree planted** by streams of water,
which **yields its fruit in season**
and whose leaf does not wither.
Whatever he does prospers.

The Lord gave me this word, and when I read it in totality, it just blew my mind.

The more I meditated on it, HE spoke and said 'seasons', which made me think about the **four** seasons we encounter every year.
Each season represents a different time of the year – a different time in our lives.

"Which yields its fruit in season" lets me know that there is a time/season for me to reap what I have sown throughout the year.

When I think about the season we are currently experiencing – fall/winter, I remembered this is the season when bears go into hibernation; the squirrels gather their nuts and birds fly south. They are all preparing themselves for **spring/summer** - the time of the year where **fruition is massive**.

God gave me this verse to reassure me/us that HE is going to open the doors of heaven and pour out blessings that we don't have room enough to receive. HE is going to perform miracles and prove Himself over and over again this year. He has had us in hibernation; we have been getting ourselves ready by tithing, praying, seeking, studying and fasting. His word says 'whatever he does prospers'! For those who don't believe, it's in the Bible; IT IS GOSPEL! HIS children **will** prosper!!! Hallelujah!

I was reading 1 Samuel with a girlfriend of mine and in verse 1:17, Eli tells Hannah to 'go in peace and may God grant you what you have asked of him'. That simple phrase 'go in peace' has stayed in my heart. It has given me such comfort in knowing that God has heard my cries and my pleas and that none of it was done in vain. HE just had to remind me that my 'season' hadn't come yet.
Praise God for being sovereign!!!

Be Blessed,
Gia

Comfort

2 Corinthians 1:4
…who comforts us in all our troubles, so that we can comfort those in any trouble with the comfort we ourselves have received from God.

1. Have you ever wondered how or why you are able to comfort those around you who may be going through a distressed moment and while you are dealing with issues of your own?
2. Have you ever wondered how or why people feel comfortable enough to come to you with their problems?
3. Have you ever wondered how or why you can speak peace into the atmosphere when chaos is going forth?

I have asked myself those very questions. And in reading the above verse, God really spoke to my heart.
I always wondered where all of this extra strength came from and why people would find comfort in speaking to me. I figured that I am just as screwed up as the next. So how indeed, was I going to shine a light anywhere?

God spoke to me and said HE is my comfort and what HE pours into me, I can release into someone else. I never stopped and thought about the fact that HE indeed does abide in us (John 15:4). Without HIM, we wouldn't be able to reassure and calm our brothers and sisters in their time of need. The reality of it is that HE empowers us every day to handle life's trials. The analogy that comes to mind is an electric current that runs through your home so that when you flip the light switch on, you have light. Without that current you would remain in the dark. (Who knew "***GE***" stood for **G**od **E**mpowers→ *brings good things to life*)

So, I would say the next time that you think you don't have a drop of encouragement left in you, think again…because God is **FOREVER**!

And I want to take this time to thank all of you out there who have encouraged me and shared Godly wisdom with me! I love you!

Be Blessed,
Gia

Amen!

Recently, I have been in a place where I am picking apart words/phrases that are used every day; sometimes loosely or with fervor. I want to know the meaning of these words/phrases that I say repeatedly.

Amen!…What is the meaning of this 4 letter word that we say at the end of our prayers?

> Side note: Notice the word has four letters; the number 4 represents supernatural happenings.

In the Webster's dictionary **Amen** is defined as a word that is used at the end of a prayer or statement to express agreement or approval.

> Another side note: 2+2 = 4…The number 2 represents union…twice the union when the word Amen is used to close out a prayer!

To know that *one* word that has such a strong and positive meaning is amazing to me. When we go to God with our petitions and we close it out by saying Amen, that means that God has heard as well as agreed to our prayers and we can leave the altar saying So Be It, because it's in God's hands now.

While reading the WORD, I have observed that this particular statement is used often → **"Then all the people shall say Amen"**. This leads me to believe that God wants **all** of His people to stand in agreement. He wants us, here on earth, to put a stamp of approval on our petitions.

Now the flip side of this (and God wants you to know this); be wary and cautious about what you go around saying Amen to, because if you are in fact agreeing and approving a lie/falsehood/deception then that puts you in a bad situation. God wants us to always be on our toes, because the enemy is everywhere and very influential. We could innocently find ourselves approving the devil…and by **NO MEANS** do we want to do that!

So because of my new findings and revelation, I would like to close this devotional out with a prayer…

Heavenly Father, I come to you with much thanksgiving in my heart and spirit. I want to thank you for your new mercies and your faithful word. I want to thank you for all that you have done for me as well as for your faithful and obedient children. Father, I also would like to thank you for your revelations and your continuous elevation. Father, I ask in YOUR NAME that you continue to increase our spiritual gifts. Lord, make our eyes and ears keener as well as our spirits more sensitive to your commands. Lord, I decree health, prosperity and obedience throughout the body of Christ. And I pray that we all keep your praises in our mouths, hearts and souls. In Jesus' Name, Amen!

Be Blessed,
Gia

Home sweet Temple

I am going to make the assumption that those who read this have a place that they reside….a place that is called *home.*

1 Corinthians 6:19-20
Do you not know that your body is the temple (the very sanctuary) of the Holy Spirit Who lives within you, Whom you have received (as a Gift) from God? You are not your own…So then, honor God and bring glory to Him in your body.

What type of presence is in your home? How do you care for your home? Do you allow others to disrespect your home?

THOUGHT: The home you live in can be compared to the *home* you provide for the Holy Spirit.

Is your body fit to be considered a temple? Does the Holy Spirit struggle to survive in your body?

God deemed our bodies as temples…a sanctuary for the Holy Spirit. I know I could go down a long list of things that you could do to defile your temple, but I think I am going to let the Holy Spirit handle that. Prior to being saved you just had a conscience. It was easier for you to do certain things without feeling bad about it. Now that you have accepted God into your life, your conscience switched from yours to ***HIS***….it wasn't to make your life harder, but to make *you better*!

I was talking to a girlfriend and we both agreed that we can see the change in our lives and our attitudes because the Holy Spirit steps in and shuts out mouths *OR* has us to use pleasant words versus harsh ones; and how else is a stranger supposed to know that you are a Christian? I don't believe in always running around claiming Christian-hood. I believe in letting your actions and conversations show where you are in Christ. I keep hearing in my head…**Actions speaks louder than words**…

We should be as determined to keep our temples free of any clutter and mess as we are about our homes. Now I know this is going to reach some people who can't go to bed until certain things are done around the house, or can't enjoy the weekend until the Saturday-morning clean-up is completed and the house is smelling and looking good. And I also know that you don't allow anyone to come and disrespect your home, I can't help but to think about Martin Lawrence, when he would quickly throw out anybody who disrespected his home. We have to have that same attitude when it comes to our bodies/temples…keep all of the junk out of it and don't allow anyone to disrespect your **home for the Holy Spirit**.

….So then, honor God and bring glory to Him in your body…..

Be Blessed,
Gia

Un-Veil-ed

I was reading 2 Corinthians 3. I read it in NIV, Amplified and Message versions; NIV titled 3:7-18 **'Lifting the Veil'** and Message titled it **'Glory of the New Covenant'**

I found it ironic that He led me to read verses that had to deal with removing the veil – preparing to become the Bride of Christ.

I asked Nichole what her first thought was when I mentioned the bride's veil being lifted by her groom at the altar. Her immediate response was a "removal of the partition for intimacy"…. the groom lifts the veil to kiss his wife for the first time under a covenant with God.

'Glory of the New Covenant'!
The moment Jesus was conceived, His life was destined to bring the world a new covenant. God blessed us with a Redeemer; so that we could confess His existence in our lives here on earth in order to have eternal lives in Heaven. When we seek Him and go into the throne room, the veil/partition for intimacy with Him is lifted; we are face to face with the King!

'Lifting the Veil'
God is unveiling us naturally and spiritually. He is bringing us to a more intimate place with Him – Bless God! It's been a slow and painful process at times, but it will all be worth it in the end. We have been under a veil to the world. He has kept us under a covering until perfection, so that when we are

revealed to the world, what they see is the Glory of God! Hallelujah!!

I can't stress enough how thankful I am to you and your advice, prayers, steadfast spirit and even your patience. I thank God for your life and for having our paths to cross.

Be Blessed,
Gia

The GLORY of the New Covenant
Un-Veil-ed part 2
Written by Nichole M. Jackson

On that day many years ago on a stony hill called Golgotha, the Savior of the world was crucified. On that day the veil that separated the Holies of Holies was rent. This was symbolic of the crucifixion and the partition that kept man from being able to fully be one with God now being removed. As God bore witness in the earth, access to Him was now available and the sin that hid us from His holiness was now removed because of the blood that was shed.

Now as believers we have all heard that scripture quoted, John 3:16 'For God so loved the world, that He gave His only begotten Son, that who so ever believe on Him should not perish." By this we know it was out of His love for us that He removed the veil that kept us from being intimate with him.

But few have failed to go into the Holies of Holies and experience the LOVE of the master. IT WAS SO HE COULD LOVE US! We often see the crucifixion as a way for us to get to God and love on God but it was really because HE wanted to love on US! The Glory of the NEW COVENANT as children-believers we get to experience the passion and love He has for His creation. Because the veil was removed, He could once again pour out His great love.

This season is a manifestation of the divine glory where God is manifesting His love for His creation through supernatural acts & divine favor.

This all being an act of love, a gift to the bride before the wedding. Prepare yourself for His return. Be expecting HIM! Live in a manner in which your conduct is pure, for you may be entertaining angles unaware and every act and word we have to give account for. Get ready for the husband man to pour out his love, and adorn yourself as the Bride of Christ.

Spring Cleaning

Jeremiah 7:5
Only if you clean up your act (the way you live, the things you do), only if you do a total spring cleaning on the way you live and treat your neighbors…

God spoke to me and said "spring cleaning" and my initial thought was OK, I need to start to do a serious cleaning to my home. But of course there was a little bit more to it!

I really didn't expect to find a verse in the Bible that referenced spring cleaning, but much to my surprise, I found one and it was relevant to His children's lives.

God had Jeremiah to tell the people of Judah that God could not move into their neighborhood until they cleaned up their act(Jer. 7:6-7); change their way of thinking and living; same thing even in 2004!
Throw away all old, non-useful, unnecessary, no-good, taking up spiritual-space thoughts, attitudes, habits and behaviors. Put it all on the curb. You don't need it anymore. It's slowing down your growth and progress.
Allow God to come in and take up residence.

I am sure we all wake up that one Saturday morning and say 'today is the day that I clean up around here'. The sun is shining brightly; the temperature is wonderful, you open the window to find there is a light breeze blowing; you (or maybe just me:) turn the radio on so that you can dance and sing around the house while you are cleaning.

You decide that you are going to throw away all of the things that haven't been used in the past year but was occupying space in attempts to make room for new and useful things. You think of things that you are going to do differently- allowing God to move throughout your spirit and remove anything that is negative and not of Him. Your spirit is awake and ready!

Spring Cleaning!

Jer 7:23…but I did say this, commanded this: "Obey Me. Do what I say and I will be your God and you will be my people. Live the way I tell you. Do what I command so that your lives will go well." (MSG)

I think the above verse in self-explanatory. I suggest that if there is ANYTHING that God has spoken and you have refused, disregarded, rejected because it wasn't easy, comfortable or you just thought that you were boss…its time to repent and obey God. I can't imagine anybody *wanting* a rough road to travel…

IT'S TIME TO CLEAN UP MY CHRISTIAN FAMILY!!

Be Blessed,
Gia

All Worship …No Worry

Psalms 34:9 Worship God if you want the best; worship opens doors to all His goodness

Proverbs 12:25 Worry weighs us down…

Last week I went to service and while my Bishop was speaking, he mentioned not to worry but to worship. And it stuck with me because I have been driving myself crazy with worrisome thoughts about my life's situations and what's to come in the future. There have been times that I have been awakened from my sleep with anxiety as to how I am going to accomplish certain tasks and the anxiety hinders my thoughts and my praises.

It seems like no sooner than I gain victory in one area of my life, another part gets shaken up and sometimes I feel that there will never be peace. As a Christian, I know to seek my Father's face when life's issues become heavy and release them all to Him. But as a human, it gets hard to do that because I am desperately trying to make good on all that I do and all that God wants me to do.

I know the enemy sits back and waits for us to beat our heads against the wall and feel like we will never make the mark…but as God had to tell me, I will tell you, **He loves us, He will not forsake us and His WORD does not return void**…so just continue to **praise Him, worship Him** and **glorify His name**…Hallelujah!

When I read Prov 12:25, I was like 'man that is so true' because when I worry and get anxious, I feel so weighed down. I don't want to be bothered with anything. And it's like the more I worry the easier it is **not to** do anything and just wallow in my own issues. And God had to pull my coat tail and remind me that I haven't been in His presence and I didn't bring my problems to **Him!**

I don't know about you, but I want the best that God has for me...I want to open the doors to His goodness...I don't want to miss out on anything that God has for me! So I will praise and worship Him at all times and rebuke the enemy when he tries to interfere!

We have to let the enemy know that he will not be victorious!! I really do feel the enemy is so heavy on the Christian body now because he knows that we are embarking upon our destiny and he is losing out. So all that he can do is have us worry and attempt to distract our thoughts and our praises. **DON'T** give him the pleasure!! **Rebuke, bind and *hinder* his plans**!

Be Blessed,
Gia

<u>Fireplace</u>

Fire – a rapid, persistent chemical change that releases heat and light and is accompanied by flame…

Matthew 3:11…He will baptize you with the Holy Spirit and fire. (NASB)

What comes to mind when you think of a fireplace?

When God gave me a vision of a fireplace, I immediately saw a brick shelter with a flame blazing on the inside. Hmmm, does that stir up something in your Spirit?

It's amazing to me that He has created our bodies to be able to contain such a high-temperature substance; that changes rapidly and persistently!

We should always want to be in His presence so that He can have free will to do with us what He sees fit…and in that there will be a purging and cleansing of anything that is in our Spirits that may be hindering our growth or maturity. If you think about it, a fireplace is at the base of a chimney. The chimney allows the smoke to be released *outside* of the home. The chimney prevents the smoke to come in contaminate your home.

I just remembered that there was a time when I was at a friend's house and they were attempting to light the fireplace. For some odd reason the smoke kept coming back inside and the soot covered everything on the first floor…not to mention, the smell of smoke was choking me. It wasn't until some time later that we realized the flue was closed and that was the reason for the disaster.

Open the flue is what God is saying and I really think I am preaching to myself right now! WOW! Allow all of the contaminates to get out of your mind, body and soul.

He is ready to turn the flame up my Christian family!

Be Blessed,
Gia

Back Seat Driver

Matthew 6:33 But seek ye **first** the kingdom of God, and his righteousness: and **all** shall be **added unto you.**

Raise your hand if you are guilty of making God the backseat driver of your life's decisions!!

I am going to be honest; I had to raise both of my hands when God brought that question to me.

God brought it to my attention and reminded me that I had Him in the backseat trying to give directions. He reminded me that I stopped seeking Him and started to seek myself.
And needless to say from the backseat He was hollering 'dead end', 'danger' and of course 'HELLO, I haven't gone anywhere'.

I was able to get a mental picture of what I was doing. It was like God was sitting in the back tapping me on the shoulder, and I would half way turn around to see what He *wanted*...**how bold of me!**
Somehow I thought that I could go down the path of life without His wisdom and guidance.

It's time that we go back to seeking His face first; its time that *we* get in the backseat and enjoy the ride that He has planned for us. His Word says that *all* **shall be added unto us...**which means He will not forsake us, but we **HAVE** to go to Him first. It's easy to think that something may be minor and that you can choose left or right...up or down...but you don't know what's to come, so how can you make these decisions **without** God giving you wisdom. He's the **Omnipotent ONE**! Praise the Lord!

If it wasn't for His grace and mercy, I can only imagine where my life would be and I don't want to take any of that for granted. His favor has shown upon my life too many times for me to tell Him to get in the back and buckle up…because truth be told, I don't know what to do or where to go or even what to say… I need Him all the time.

Praise God for loving us first!

Be Blessed,
Gia

Holy Ordained Promises Executed

Romans 5:5 ...and hope does not disappoint, because the love of God has been poured out within our hearts through the Holy Spirit who was given to us.

Psalms 119:116 Sustain me according to Your word, that I may live: And do not let me be ashamed of my hope.

I receive daily verses from a website and the one today was Romans 5:5. I thought to myself that this is relevant to the Christian body because if you are anything like me…you hope!

I realized that I say the word 'hope' so much and maybe even at times loosely, that I knew I needed to get out of this verse what God is trying to tell me. He is saying it's OK to hope! Hallelujah!
I couldn't believe that 'hoping' was something done in the Biblical days and He granted it according to His will!!
We do it now so much that I think we subconsciously snatch away what it means to 'hope' in a Christian way.

> Hope – to have confidence; trust; to look forward with confidence or expectation

So if you take the definition of hope and think about your prayers and the desires of your heart…that means that you have **confidence and trust** that God is going to bless. The definition also mentions that hoping for something means you are looking **forward** with expectation.

> Side note – stop looking behind you; stop looking in your past…its time to look forward with expectations!

The second verse that I referenced states not being ashamed of your hope. Don't allow the enemy to discourage you…it's not worth losing out on a blessing because of the enemy's whispers and mind games.
It's very easy for you to get disheartened when you take your hopes and dreams to those who don't believe, so guard your mouth and don't throw your pearls before swine.

His word says hope **does not disappoint**…that is powerful right there!

I appreciate each one of you taking your time to read my devotionals and I think that the best way that I can close this, is to quote Jesse Jackson - **KEEP HOPE ALIVE!**

Be Blessed,
Gia

King's Kid

Rev 5:12 Saying in a loud voice, Deserving is the Lamb, Who was sacrificed, to receive all the power and riches and wisdom and might and honor and majesty (glory, splendor) and blessing!

Rev 17:14 …and the Lamb will triumph over them; for He is Lord of lords and King of kings….

Do you *really* know **and** understand who you belong to? You are a child of the Most High!

I can remember when I was growing up and I was being introduced to others, I was always 'Clunie's kid' and I can remember feeling proud of whom I belonged to.
I felt that I could walk around with my head high because of who my father was at the same time being mindful of things that I said or did *because of* who my father was. I never wanted to disappoint him.

Now that I have given my life to Christ, I have grown to know who my **Father** is. Being a child of God has brought on a feeling that I can't even begin to describe. I am a child of God – the King of kings!!
I can hold my head high because I know that my Father is miraculous. He can do all things, **(Luke 1** [37]For nothing is impossible with God.") There is nothing that is impossible for Him to do – NOTHING!!
Because of Who He is, I want to represent Him well. I don't want someone to look at me and say is that the *'King's Kid'* acting like that?

Responsibility most definitely comes with being a child of God, but so do blessings, favors, miracles, grace, mercy (etc.)…..so I think being a responsible Christian has its perks.

I just have to note that there is a verse that keeps popping up and I am mainly speaking to those who are going through some trials…Psalm 46:10 Be still and know that I am God. It may look like Pharaoh and his armies are gaining on you, but know that God has a divine plan for you to be free and will drown your enemy.

    Hey, you are the *King's Kid!*

Be Blessed,
Gia

Go Home!

Mark 5:19
Jesus did not let him [the man from whom he had cast out demons] come with him, but said**, "Go home** to your family and tell them how much the Lord has done for you, and how he has had mercy on you."

Luke 22:32
But I have prayed for thee, that thy faith fail not; and when thou art converted, **strengthen thy brethren**.

I have come to realize that it's real easy to speak about God and give testimony to those that are already saved; the challenge comes when you have to witness to those who grew up with you or raised you **and** know *all* of your dirt.

YOUR FAMILY can be the hardest people to witness to. These people can barely remember what they ate yesterday, but they can recall everything *wrong* that you did. And I know this is true, because I was guilty of reminding my saved family of their past lives.

I believe there was a reason why Jesus told the man to go home to his family and tell them about His mercy. Jesus knew that it wasn't an easy task. This man probably did some unimaginable things because he was filled with demonic spirits and his family probably had cast him out. He had to return to his family and speak on what the Lord had done for him and go up against any doubt that might have come his way.

Don't allow the views of the unbelievers to discourage you, if they choose to remind you of your past transgressions. Choose to stand firm on God's Word. God saved you and He can save them!

If you could drink more than a fish, couldn't go two days without sex, every other word was a curse word, laid in the bed every Sunday morning, never picked up a Bible and flipped somebody the bird if they cut you off on the highway…and now you have turned away from that old, destructive behavior and are still striving to be an upright Christian…believe me, they are noticing it all.

Continue to encourage your family. Your conversation and your consistent actions will win them over.

Plant the seed and let God bring the increase! (1 Corinthians 3 [6]I planted the seed, Apollos watered it, but God made it grow.)

Be Blessed,
Gia

Show and Tell

John 6:14 When the people saw the sign (miracle) that Jesus had performed, they began saying, Surely and beyond a doubt this is the Prophet Who is to come into the world!

I am sure that all of you had to be a part of the show and tell when you were in elementary school. For the most part this was a time set aside for you to show your classmates what you possessed. It was a time that you could show your friends that you actually owned this particular thing (especially those kids who never wanted to believe and constantly doubted). After you stood before your peers and let all of their eyes gleam, you were able to sit down and say 'I told you so!'

Christian family, we are in the season of show and tell. God is performing miracles to show His people what it is that He *really* possess.

For those that have doubted God's power…get ready for a show!

God is going to stand before His children and perform miracles after miracles!
Not that He has to… but because He loves us that much, He wants us to know of His marvelous powers! He wants to open eyes, hearts, minds and souls of those who haven't surrendered their lives to receive Him.

God has sat among us telling us what He has for His children and what He can do and some of us have not been so eager to believe. We may have been simply sitting back waiting on God to prove Himself before we praise His Name. **PRAISE HIM NOW!! REJOICE NOW!!** He is going to do it! His word does not return to Him void.
Start jumping and screaming right now....whew! Praise God!

And after our eyes are gleaming and staring in amazement, God is going to say 'I told you so!' Hallelujah!

Be Blessed,
Gia

Recall

Romans 12:[12]Be joyful in hope, patient in affliction, faithful in prayer.

I was reading Romans 12 and this particular verse stuck out the most because I remembered that I wrote on hope, patience and prayer within the past year. I asked God what was it that He was showing me, so He led me back to the devotional titled '3=1' and this is the part that God led me to…
… While I was meditating on the Word, HE had me to look up the word 'mature'….
James 1:4 Perseverance must finish its work so that you may be **mature** and complete, not lacking anything…

MATURITY – reaching a desired or final condition; ripe…when I read the word ripe, The Lord said 'fruit'…fruit can be consumed in its mature stage…The Lord can consume us in our mature stage…

God said 'its picking time'…Praise God!
My Christian family we have treaded through some rough waters, traveled up some rough mountains and survived the barren desert! Our time is now!

We remained patient while God worked on our behalves; we hoped and prayed through it all…whew! We kept our Christianity *and* sanity while the enemy put the press on.

God said open your mouth and let out a holler of victory!! Release all of the anxiety that has developed in your spirit, because God is opening the windows of heaven for you!

REJOICE!!!
HALLELUJAH!!!

This is a short and sweet devotional to let you know that we have arrived! Bless the Name of Jesus!

> **Note:** God is leading me to ask for any testimonies that happen within the next month, so that there is a written record of God's blessings.

Be Blessed,
Gia

Desiring God's Desires…

Psalm 21
²You have given him his heart's desire and have not withheld the request of his lips. Selah [pause, and think of that]!

Question: How often do you desire what **God wants for you life** vs. your *own* desires?

That question hit me like a brick when it was mentioned. I had to think back to my prayers and my daily thoughts and try to remember if I ask God for *His* desires on my life??

There have been times that I got to the point after I have prayed on something for a while that I would say "God, YOUR will be done"…but I have to be honest and say it wasn't my initial prayer.

I know the Bible says you have not because you ask not (James 4:2….You do not have, because you do not ask God.) And because my thoughts are not as high as God's, of course the things I ask for are mediocre in comparison to what HE **can** give – and not even in material form but spiritually.

We were created for His pleasure and what we receive while we are here is really for His glory. Yes, we enjoy all the blessings; but all the praises go to Him.

Can you imagine if you asked for God's desires on your life??

Can you imagine if your heart's desire was God's desire for you??

I know it can be scary and overwhelming to think about where God wants to take us and what He wants from us, so sometimes we might purposely not seek God for His will.

Well, I will like to throw a challenge out there (for all of my daring folks :)…with an open and purged heart. Take a moment and ask God for His desires concerning you…

Seek Him first for *His desires*!

Be Blessed,
Gia

Characteristics

Patience of Job
Job 2:10…."Shall we indeed accept good from God and not accept adversity?" In all this Job did not sin with his lips.

Heart of David
Acts 13:22 …He also testified and said 'I have found David the son of Jesse, a man after my heart, who will do all MY will'

Noah's Obedience
Genesis 7: 5 Noah did according to all that the LORD had commanded him

All Praises to the Lord!

I pray that the Spirit moves within you as soon as you read the above scriptures.
The WORD that God has given me in those three subtitles is potent.

In the previous devotional I wrote (Desiring God's Desires), I challenged you to pray and ask God what His desires for your life.

Well, I took that challenge and this is what He gave me this morning. It came to me in bits and pieces, but now that I see it altogether I am happy that I took on the challenge!

I am going to present it to you in the manner that God gave it to me, and see if you catch it in your spirit!

FIRST
I am certain that you know what Job endured and I have to admit that I always felt that Job was a whole lot better than I! I never felt that I had that much strength or patience to take on such turmoil and tragedy and *still* be able to praise God. It's very easy to take all the good that God has to offer, but when adversity hits, my spirit would immediately get jumpy. He said that He wants me to have patience and peace through it all and **continue** to glorify His name…He's deserving of it.

SECOND
He raised up David to be king and said that he would do His will. There are goals that God desires to be accomplished. Recently, I have joined in with others to complete goals that God has set before us. And it wasn't an immediate five-year plan; but outlining what God expected of us weekly (nothing hard or complex); and let us **rejoice** in God's purpose/desire for our lives. As long as we are on our ordained paths, there can only be victory at the end!

THIRD
We are currently living in a world where this is much distraction surrounding us. If we aren't careful and mindful, we can certainly get caught up in it. Seek for God's favor; turn away from the riff-raff and focus on what God wants from you. If you ask me, **Noah's obedience** most definitely saved his life! Noah knew

the fear of God and didn't include himself in the behavior of his peers and because of it he found favor in the LORD (Gen 6:8 But Noah found favor in the eyes of the LORD) and his life was spared.

When I thought about these characteristics, I saw that Noah was a combination of Job *and* David….no wonder why he received **FAVOR!**

This isn't all that God wants from us, so as we continue to pray for His direction…favor will lie ahead in our paths.

> **Side note: God pointed out the fact that the last scripture I referenced is from Genesis (the beginning)…it's a new beginning! Hallelujah!**

Be Blessed,
Gia

Love Thy Neighbor

Leviticus 19
[18]You shall not take revenge or bear any grudge against the sons of your people, but you shall **love your neighbor as yourself**. I am the LORD.

Let's be completely honest…how many of you have a *hard time* with this particular verse?

We live in a world where we have to deal with attitudes, backstabbing and betrayal and it is not always easy to 'love thy neighbor'.

Not only are we expected to love our neighbor, *but* we have to love them *as* we love ourselves! I have to be straightforward and say that is a challenge for me. I love myself even when I disappoint myself! However it is difficult for me to love someone that has hurt me. I can not have a grudge or take revenge, all I am supposed to do is love them!

Christians are expected to conduct themselves in ways that were not considered prior to being saved. Most of the time 'humility' is the name of the game. We have to keep the snappy comments to ourselves and allow God to deal with the person – not always the first thought or the easiest approach.

Being a believer of Christ and being filled with the Holy Spirit, we have to learn to let God be God! He knows who is deceiving us before we know it. Sometimes I think He allows the situation to occur just to see how we are going to handle ourselves.

He is saying to the body to purge and rid yourself of that demon. Don't allow yourself to lose hold of the cross and go against what He has taught you. God is big enough to handle all of your battles and here's a secret – He can handle it better than you could do any day!

Love *and* **pray** for your enemies. And more importantly, love them as you love yourself. If you cherish and treasure yourself - cherish and treasure them as well, they are God's creations just like you.

Be Blessed,
Gia

Walking with Armour

Ephesians 6:11
Put on the full armour of God, so that you will be able to stand firm against the schemes of the devil.

God gave me a vision of me speaking to a congregation. The name of the sermon was 'Walking it Out'. During the sermon, I could see myself emulating a person walking and every time they wanted to get tired of their walk and turn away, there was an angel to turn them back around. Then I saw myself covered in armour and on the front on the chest plate it read **'On Assignment'** and on the back it read **'From God'**

I began to think about the armour that we wear - why is it really necessary? God gave me a mental picture of the 'before the fight' and 'after the fight'. Before the fight, the armour is nice and shiny with no markings. After the fight, the armour is banged up! God said if **I** didn't cover you out there on the battlefield, what do *you* think you would look like?
He is a necessary covering when going up against the enemy, because as you know the enemy will immediately pounce on whomever he can. The enemy cares nothing about you, so he will tear you up, beat you down and throw you out to the wolves. The **full armour of God** protects you!

The armour will carry you through the rough waters and over the obstacles, and bring you up to your reward.

Don't get wary and tired! Don't give up! Don't turn away!
(Isaiah 40:31…They will run and not get tired, they will walk and not become weary)

Part of the armour is strength, there is no getting TIRED! (Eph 6:15 your feet fitted with the readiness that comes from the gospel of peace)

Part of the armour is faith, there is no WORRYING! (Eph 6:16..take up the shield of faith, with which you can extinguish all the flaming arrows of the evil one.)

Part of the armour is victory, there is no DEFEAT! (Eph 6:17 Take up the helmet of salvation and the sword of the Spirit, which is the word of God); (Isaiah 55:11 So shall My word be that goeth forth out of My mouth; It shall not return unto Me void)

In closing, I asked God why was there wording on the chest plate? He said "Its for the enemy to see that another one of His children is on the battlefield with an agenda (**On Assignment**), and when they get past the enemy, he can see Who sent them (**From God**)"!!

Be Blessed,
Gia

Printed in the United States
22298LVS00004B/7-51